written
and
illustrated
by
Wes Seeliger
Foreword by Keith Miller

PIONEER VENTURES Publishers
Houston, Texas

Printed in the United States of America.
Library of Congress catalog card number: 72-96685

ISBN 0-915321-00-9

FOR JENNY,
My Pioneer Wife

THANKS, PARDNER

These pioneers have helped with the book. Thanks are extended to:

Professor Decherd H. Turner, Jr., Southern Methodist University, Dallas, Texas, for reading the manuscript and making helpful suggestions.

Mrs. Patty Strine, Houston, Texas, for typing the manuscript.

Mr. James E. Hill, Houston, Texas, for his technical assistance.

The pioneer parishioners of The Episcopal Church of the Advent, Houston, Texas, for their encouragement.

Wes Seeliger

Houston, Texas

FOREWORD

Western Theology is a sharp satire which
reveals in a bright (and sometimes garish) light
some of the most closed and demeaning behavior
patterns and heresies of the institutional church.
Wes Seeliger's pictures are vivid and confront-
ing. If you are not accustomed to satire as a
medium of communication, you may think this
entire book is a horrible sacrilege. (And I'm not
sure some of it isn't.) But if you try to keep in
mind that it is a kind of joke that carries a
serious load, you probably won't be offended at
the handling of "sacred concepts," and you will
likely be in for a stimulating and thought-
provoking experience.

There is no doubt in my mind that we
in the church are guilty of the basic charges
made against "settler Christianity." At least I am.
I like to think of myself as a pioneer type, but
even the way I feel when I say it tells me there
is lots of settler mentality in my pleasure at not
feeling like one. I suspect that many readers

will feel that Wes has "gone too far" with
some of his analogies, but sometimes it takes
vivid pictures to make us consider what *we* think.

I hope thousands of Christian laymen
and ministers will read this book and think
about what the Christian life and message mean
to them. By using this as a kickoff point for
study, a group could do research on the various
concepts dealt with in the book and find out
what they believe the trinity, the church, the
ministry, the Christian life-style, etc. look like
"on the hoof."

Of course if you're not a real compul-
sive, you may just want to enjoy the book. But if
you do study it, you may wind up disturbed,
and you may come out at a place Wes Seeliger
didn't even mention. But I don't think that will
bother him, since according to *Western Theology*
"Wild Red" will be with you on the trail.

Keith Miller

PREFACE

"How can anyone who is serious about life call himself a Christian? The church is a nursery full of frightened, immature people who want to hang on to the status quo. Belief in God is superstition. Clergymen belong in zoos. The church is dying and I say good riddance. The whole business stinks."

So spoke one of my friends. He was angry. One of his close friends had been admitted to the State Hospital for shock treatments following a "religious" experience.

An isolated example? Not really. My friend speaks for more people than we clergy would like to imagine. And how many regular churchgoers secretly suspect the church is a dead horse? How many feel no sense of life and power in the church? Perhaps they wouldn't speak as bluntly as my friend, but if pressed they couldn't tell you what the Christian faith means to them.

What's the trouble? Why is the church hitting on only four cylinders? There are a dozen answers to this question. They range from "dull sermons" to "being out of touch with the 20th Century." There is truth in all these answers.

But one of our problems has to do with pictures, or mental images. What pictures come to mind when the words Christian, God, Church, Clergyman, Christ are mentioned? What

graphic images do these concepts convey?
What does the word "God" mean to my friend
who says belief in God is superstition? What
does he see in his mind's eye when he closes
his eyes and thinks, "church"?

One thing is clear. We can't rely on
words alone. It's time to dust off the photo album
and compare "life pictures." (Note: Jesus was
doing this with parables 2000 years before
Marshall McLuhan was born.)

Western Theology is a picture book. It
was born out of agony and ecstasy. The agony of
using a vocabulary that said life to me, but death
to many others. The ecstasy of seeing people
come alive when they could grasp new images
of the Christian faith.

Western Theology is a cartoon sketch of
two spirits: the settler spirit and the pioneer
spirit.

The settler spirit is my picture of
unfaith: the closed life. The settler is the unad-
venturesome soul who dies by inches in his cast
iron world.

The pioneer spirit is my picture of faith:
the open life. The pioneer is the man who is
totally alive. He stakes his life on promises. He is
responsive to demands. Like Abraham, he packs
up and takes off for parts unknown. He lives
with the humility of a man constantly in danger,
and the joy of a man who sleeps under the stars

and sees a new horizon each morning.

The settler-pioneer categories have nothing to do with a man's occupation or external circumstances. A guy working on a doll buggy assembly line may be filled with the pioneer spirit. A high wire acrobat or astronaut may be settler to the bone. These categories describe attitudes, or types of faith, not externals. To be a settler is to clutch life. To be a pioneer is to go full steam ahead.

These categories apply to the church as well as to individuals. The settler and pioneer spirits battle within the church.

The settler spirit is very much with us. Its symptoms: fear of all change, the desire to "protect" God, the return to Old Time Religion (i.e., 19th Century revivalism), religion as a retreat from a dangerous world, and so on.

But across the barbed wire fence is the pioneer spirit. It goes under many names, but perhaps "renewal of the church" is most common. Its signs are legion: theological and liturgical renewal; the church as maker rather than victim of history; the lay movement; investing in people rather than real estate; democratization of the ecclesiastical machine; the clergy association movement, etc.

Western Theology is a picture album of these spirits as they stand nose to nose across no-man's land.

The author is optimistic. The pioneer spirit will win. We will have our pioneer church before the end of this century. The old covered wagon is on the way. You can hear the wheels creaking.

Western Theology is a call to side with the winners. To move out—take a chance—live dangerously. We all have both settler and pioneer in us. May "Wild Red" (The Holy Spirit) blast the settler and fan the pioneer spark. For this is a great time to be on the wagon train. Let us leave our sterile old ghost towns and risk it all following the wild, surprising God of the Bible. The God who goes by the name I WILL BE WHAT I WILL BE.

(See Exodus, Chapter 3)

Wes Seeliger

CHURCH—COURTHOUSE

In Settler Theology the church is the courthouse. The old frame structure stands in the middle of the town square. It is topped by a weather vane that squeaks as it points the direction of the wind. The hands on the courthouse clock are frozen in place by years of neglect and rust. Worm-eaten planks confirm the feeling that time has stopped. Small windows with heavy shutters wall out the sunshine. This makes the edifice easy to defend, but quite dark inside. The solid oak doors are kept locked except during business hours. Only pigeons lining the roof offer any sign of life. But they, of course, are most unwelcome. Each year the courthouse gets a fresh coat of whitewash. This is done just before the Mayor's annual courthouse council.

The black doormat bears the command to "Wipe Feet Before Entering." Branching out from the long, cold, creaky corridor on the first floor are the offices. The first office is that of the Tax-Assessor-Collector. Over his huge steel safe is a sign lettered in gold, "Give A Tithe And Your Business Will Thrive."

Down the hall is a heavy door which is kept locked. This is the door to the archives room which contains relics of the pioneer days and houses a strong concrete vault. *The Almanac* is kept in it. This book tells of the pioneer days before folks settled down. It is filled with wild tales of adventure, excitement, challenge. The town fathers are cautious with *The Almanac*. Such tales could upset the harmony of the town and would, perhaps, raise questions about the courthouse. Hence the locked door.

The large room at the end of the corridor is the meeting place of the County Commissioners, the town's most prominent citizens. Known as the "Mayor's Boys," they are the pillars of the courthouse. These solid citizens argue far into the night about how the courthouse should be run. But their arguments change nothing. The Settler City Charter assures that. No changes may be made without a unanimous vote ten years in a row. And then the Mayor can bust it with a veto.

A wrought-iron staircase leads to the second floor. Here are the courtroom and the Mayor's office.

Lining the lawn of the fortress-like courthouse are markers honoring prominent citizens, especially past Bank Presidents. In the middle of the lawn, surrounded by "Keep Off The Grass" signs, is a granite statue of the Mayor, inscribed:

THE HONORABLE ALPHA O. MEGA.
SUPREME BEING OF SETTLER CITY
B.C. Zero

The courthouse is the settler's symbol of law, order, tradition, stability, and, most important, security.

CHURCH—WAGON TRAIN

In Pioneer Theology the church is a wagon train. It is always on the move—over mountains and through dark valleys, in fair weather and storm. No place is its home.

The wagon train is not comfortable or safe. The wagons are bandaged with bailing wire, pitted by arrows, patched and worn. Yet they creak along.

The train does not hesitate to move into new, hostile territory. The pioneers gladly trade safety for obedience to the insistent voice of the Trail Boss.

The wagon train is a sight to behold. Every type of wagon can be found in the endless line. The pioneers welcome diversity. Who can argue styles and brand names when there is a new world to explore? Each pioneer knows his well-being depends on the good of all.

Life can be hectic. There are rivers to ford, wagons to pull out of the mud. The boredom of the plain. The excitement of danger. But through it all the pioneers are driven by the vision of what is yet to be, and by obedience to the tasks of the day.

The pioneers eat, sleep, love, fight, and die on the wagons. The wagon train is not where one goes—it is where one lives.

Although they cherish land already explored, the pioneers never glorify the wagon's ruts. They love the past because it has brought them to the present. But they realize that to live in the past is to give up pioneering.

GOD—MAYOR

In Settler Theology God is the mayor. His office is on the second floor of the courthouse. The shutters on his windows are kept closed lest a mortal see his face. This makes the place quite dark and musty. His office walls are lined with dust-covered books whose yellow pages tell of past glories. Under a "Repent" sign is the Mayor's leather chair. He keeps a glass of water in one of his desk drawers. In it are his false teeth. A strand of barbed wire (symbol of the taming of the frontier) is in another. On his heavy mahogany desk is a gold nameplate, THE HONORABLE ALPHA O. MEGA. A cabinet contains the file of the Courthouse Committee on Unsettler Activities. The Mayor has a telegraph receiver which permits settlers downstairs to send him messages. A large bronze spittoon, which the Mayor has never been known to miss, completes the office decor.

The Mayor is a sight to behold. From his black bowler to his fancy boots, he is totally other than all that is. He puffs fat expensive cigars. The 24-carat diamond on his little finger sparkles in the office gloom. He is predictable, punctual, and pugnacious. Above all, he hates to be contradicted.

Often, the Mayor's eagle eye peers through a broken shutter slat. Nothing escapes his gaze.

His all-seeing eye notes the movements, thoughts, and actions in Settler City.

The Mayor's main concerns are peace and quiet. That's why he sends the Sheriff to check on strangers who ride into town. Strangers tend to confuse settlers with questions.

Nothing happens unless the Mayor gives his OK. He is the first cause of everything. The Mayor controls the courthouse, which in turn runs the town.

A hand-lettered scroll hangs in the Mayor's office. It is a copy of his inaugural address:

I'm Mayor O. Mega, the judge of
    this town
You settlers watch it, I don't mess
    around
So keep all my laws or in hell
    you'll stew
You better obey me or here's what
    I'll do:

I'll send my Sheriff to deliver the blow
You'll be spread-eagled forever on my
    anthill below
As the rawhide shrinks and you let out
    a groan
You'll wish you had trusted my
    Sheriff alone.

Such rough stuff on my part may seem
    reprehensible
And even to me it's incomprehensible

But don't judge me harshly; please
    trust me, my brother
It's tough for me to be "totally other."

But you sweet settlers who keep your
    nose clean
Will know in the next world I'm not
    such a fiend
You'll cash in your chips in the Sweet
    By-and-By
At that great Golden Ranch way off
    in the sky.

If you keep my rules and don't give me
    no sass
You'll have order in town and peace at
    the last
So partners beware—I'm makin' a list
Some will see blessings, but others
    my fist.

                Alpha O. Mega
                Supreme Being

GOD—TRAIL BOSS

In Pioneer Theology God is Mr. J. Hova, the Trail Boss. "Mr. J.," as the pioneers call him, is a tough hombre. He rides hard. He has big teeth, huge hands, and size 13 feet. His tall frame is topped by a black hat. (White hats are worn only by dudes from back East.) Mr. J. keeps a bottle of whiskey in his weather-beaten saddle bags. This is for medicinal purposes only—naturally. Mounted on his horse, he is a sight for sore eyes.

Mr. J. runs the show, no doubt about it. But he's not stand-offish. He lives, eats, fights, and sleeps with his men. He is nearer to them than their own boots. Their well-being is his concern. Without him things just would not be the way they are.

The Trail Boss keeps the wagons moving and the pioneers jumping. Seems like folks never get to rest. Mr. J. is always hollering about something. As soon as one hill is crossed, one task done, one horizon reached, he starts raving about new adventures. He never gets tired.

Mr. J. is not above getting downright mean—when the pioneers need it. If the pioneers get soft and want to turn back, POW! If they long for the old homestead, Mr. J. starts cussing. If necessary, he slugs the pioneers who want to chicken out on themselves and their fellow pioneers. But even his fist is an expression of his concern. Somehow the pioneers know this. Even guys who get it on the jaw. They know deep down that it's better to be a sore, alive pioneer than a comfortable, dead settler.

But the Trail Boss isn't all vinegar. He has his tender side. He never gives up on the pioneers. He cares for all people, settlers

and pioneers alike. He is gentle with the wounded. His sense of humor is tremendous. Mr. J. and the Buffalo Hunter stay up late at night thinking of new, unusual ways to startle the settlers.

He isn't easy to understand. But wherever he goes, life follows. Full life. Adventuresome life. Where he goes, hope for a new future is born.

The Trail Boss is hard to get to know. He doesn't come on command like a trained puppy. And he rarely shows his hand, just a few cards at a time. Yet his call to move out comes to everyone. Where there is a restless desire to move into the unknown, to blaze new trails for all men, to live it up—there is the Trail Boss. Even if the folks don't see his face or know precisely what to call him. What makes a pioneer is not some fancy dude theory about the Trail Boss. What makes a pioneer is the burning desire to move out.

The Trail Boss likes to mumble to himself as he rides along. He makes up ditties. His favorite goes like this:

They call me Elohim
Jehovah and To Be,
But names don't mean a thing, 'cause
I'm such a mystery.

I am what I am now,
I'll be what I will be;
Come on, my friend, get on the trail
For all men should be free!

JESUS—SHERIFF

In Settler Theology Jesus is the Sheriff. He is tall, blond, and handsome. His soft blue eyes and neatly trimmed beard make hearts flutter. His white clothes and white hat are accented by his gold handcuffs, belt buckle, and badge. His matched six-shooters have pearl handles.

The Sheriff's candle-lit office is always tidy. No spittoon, no ashtrays, no snuff boxes clutter the place. White curtains hide the window bars. The sign over the door reads, "Support Your Local Sheriff."

The Sheriff is sent by the Mayor to enforce the rules. The Sheriff's job is to see that nothing disturbs the tranquility of Settler City. He 'saves' the settlers by offering security. This means reassuring settlers that the Mayor is in the courthouse. It also involves preventative measures, and punishment for law-breakers.

The Sheriff uses three tactics. One is the "sugar method." By being a perfect example of sweetness, love, kindness, and lawfulness, the Sheriff shines before the stiff-necked settlers. With his blue eyes and sweet smile, he melts their hearts. Who can resist striving to follow such a fine, wholesome example? This tactic is used in the Protestant section of town.

In Catholic neighborhoods the Sheriff makes the settlers feel guilty. He wears long handle underwear made of mule hair. He lets the tough guys beat him up and then he walks around with a black eye. When the settlers see how hard the Sheriff works and how much he suffers on their behalf, they feel ashamed and try to shape up. Though the Sheriff never complains, the settlers know he is a man of sorrows. Like the mayor always says, "Guilty settlers are obedient settlers."

If both these soft sell methods fail, there's always the hard sell—Operation Boot Hill. It goes like this: Most settlers believe they will not really be dead when they die (they'll be kind of dead, of course, but not plumb dead). They live in dread of "The Last Roundup." Nobody wants to wind up on the Mayor's anthill. This makes most settlers easy to manage. Though the Sheriff, being a nice man, doesn't dwell on the last roundup, he mentions it when necessary. All he has to do is take out his guitar and sing his warning. It goes like this:

(Tune: "What A Friend We Have In Jesus")
What a Sheriff in the jailhouse
Keeping order all the time
And you outside agitators
Put rebellion from your minds
If you break the Mayor's ordinance
You will have to pay the fine
So fit in the mold, my brothers
You must walk the narrow line.

When your earthly race is over
And to this old world you die
You'll be glad you kept your nose clean
When you're settled in the sky
Never make your own decisions
Better be a passive guy
If you don't obey the rule book
In the next world you will fry.

Like the Mayor always says, "If they won't join ya', lick 'em."

But the Sheriff's job is not as hard as it seems. In their better moments, all settlers realize that harmony is the pearl of great price.

The Sheriff is not alone. He has two deputies: Billy James and Dr. Billy G. Kidd.

Deputy Billy James, a distant cousin of Jesse, is in charge of three law enforcement agencies. First, there is the Courthouse Committee of Un-settler Activities. This committee is on the lookout for any complaints which might mar the niceness of Settler City. Members report on their fellow settlers. They don't exactly spy—let's just say they're very observant.

Next comes the Christapo. The Christapo is a group of hand-picked agents responsible for preventing the bank tellers from giving out any wooden nickels. They report directly to the Mayor.

Last but not least is the Calvary Cavalry. This band is in charge of patrolling the outskirts of Settler City and watching for strangers. Each night the Calvary Cavalry goes on its silent search. This makes the settlers sleep better.

The Sheriff's other deputy is Dr. Billy G. Kidd. Kidd is an undercover agent. They call him "doctor" because he runs a travelling medicine show. He covers the territory in his fancy medicine wagon.

The settlers love Dr. Billy. Wherever he goes, a crowd of settlers gathers in his huge tent. When the crowd quiets, Billy starts his pitch. It always begins the same way—"*The Almanac says....*" Billy then reads a few carefully chosen bits from *The Almanac*. He describes all the aches and pains a body could possibly have. Then, with everyone's mind on his own rheumatism, Billy launches Part Two of his act. Holding up a bottle of "Dr. Billy's Cure-All Tonic," he shouts:

> *One swallow of this*
> *Will cure all your woes*
> *It'll rattle your bones*
> *From your head to your toes*
>
> *So raise up your hand*
> *And come get it, brother*
> *If you miss this chance*
> *You ain't gettin' another.*

Hands go up. Customers walk down. Dr. Billy always does good business because his tonic packs a wallop. The settlers love it. The Sheriff loves it, too. Billy keeps everyone so high they forget the boredom and routine of Settler City. By focusing everyone's attention on his home remedy, Billy helps the Sheriff keep peace. Yessir! Billy and the Sheriff are real close buddies.

Things are under control in Settler City. That's the way the settlers like it.

JESUS—SCOUT

In Pioneer Theology Jesus is the Scout. He rides ahead to find out which way the pioneers should go. The scout has a chest like a barrel of nails. He wears buckskin and has a black hat with a red feather. He could easily be mistaken for Pancho Villa, but his nose is bigger. It could be legend, but the pioneers claim he once picked up the back end of a wagon by himself.

Not much is known about his early life except that he hails from a ghost town called Dry Gulch. Folks tease him and say, "Can anything good come out of Dry Gulch?" But he takes it on the chin. Legend has it he was born in a livery stable behind the Buffalo Head Hotel. His ma named him Joshua. The pioneers call him Josh for short.

There's something special about Josh. For some reason he seems more alive than most folks. He always looks life straight in the eye and says YES! Nothing scares him. He's always ready for a new day of adventure. He's also the first one to dance when someone has a fiddle and a jug. Yet, when the Trail Boss needs a job done that takes guts, Josh is ready to go.

By observing Josh, the pioneers learn what pioneering is all about. He is the embodiment of raw courage, love of adventure, obedience to the Trail Boss, strength—you name it.

Josh is not just a scout, he is *the* scout. The pioneers talk about Josh like "Scout" was his last name. Sometimes folks just holler "Scout" when they need Josh.

The pioneers love and admire Josh, but there's always something disturbing about his presence. You see, there's a settler hidden in even the bravest pioneer. This invisible settler within keeps whispering, "It ain't worth it, play it safe, turn back, I'm tired, I'm scared." When he looks at the hot, barren trail, a pioneer is mighty tempted to listen to that voice. He starts longing for the good old days back in town. A hot bath. A soft bed. A mirror and shaving soap. He thinks to himself, "Better fed than dead."

Then comes Josh, and the pioneer is reminded of what he already knows: that life on the trail is LIFE. There ain't no other. All else is death. Josh shows the pioneers that the Trail Boss can be trusted in storm and sunshine. But this call to move out, come hell or high water, is always disturbing.

Of course, the settlers can't stand Josh. They think he is too wild and uncouth. He might lead their young ones astray. That's why they sic the Sheriff on him every time he rides into town. Josh feels sorry for the settlers, but you can't *force* anybody to become a pioneer. You know the saying about leading a horse to water.

Josh is the great trailblazer. He cuts the trail over mountains and through valleys, in good times and in bad. His spirit is contagious.

Just seeing Josh ride by on his horse, Advent, is enough to stir the heart of the weariest pioneer. His presence creates a stampede in the soul.

Josh and the Trail Boss work hand in hand. In fact, the pioneers say, "If you've seen one, you've seen 'em both." Josh shows that the pioneer life of openness, daring, and adventure is not just *one* way to live. It is what life is all about. The pioneer life *is* LIFE.

HOLY SPIRIT

HOLY SPIRIT—SALOON GIRL

In Settler Theology the Holy Spirit is Miss Dove, the Saloon Girl. She runs the Olive Branch Saloon.

      Miss Dove is quite a gal. Very appealing! She could charm the bumps off a wart hog. Her dancing costumes brighten drab Settler City. She has a costume for each season—purple, white, red, and green.

      The Olive Branch is right next door to the Sheriff's office. It's always dark inside. The soft evening sun filters through colored glass windows. Candlelight completes the warm, cozy interior. Over the heavy mahogany bar is a picture of Eve in the Garden of Eden. The settlers love that picture. Eve ain't got much on.

      Norman Spill, the Bartender, serves warm milk and the nonalcoholic kind of whiskey. (Note to settlers: Just as there are two kinds of wine, alcoholic and nonalcoholic, so there are two kinds of whiskey.) Norman is the most popular man in town. Folks love Old Norm. He has a good word for everyone. He listens to tales of woe by the hour, but from him never is heard a discouraging word. He tells folks to think positively, to look for the silver lining. Miss Dove couldn't do without him.

The Olive Branch is the settlers' favorite hangout. They go there when life gets dull, or when they feel lonely. Miss Dove tickles them under the chin and makes everything OK again. That's her job. To comfort the settlers and help them forget their troubles.

Miss Dove gives a special performance each Wednesday night. How the settlers look forward to it! With everyone seated, the saloon lights go down. A hush falls over the audience. Then the announcer, in his smooth voice, says: "And now, ladies and gentlemen, the Olive Branch proudly presents the nightingale of Settler City—Miss Dove, the comforter."

With good old Norm furnishing the accompaniment on his harmonica, Miss Dove slowly lifts her eyes and begins her sweet song:

(Tune: "Rock of Ages")
Listen while I sing this tune
In the Olive Branch Saloon
With the candles burning low
I will peace of mind bestow

Put your trust in sweet Miss Dove
While you drink in all this love.

Raise your hands up in the air
Close your eyes and say a prayer
Let your worries fall away
Turn your dark night into day
Don't be troubled or cast down
Trust the Sheriff of this town.

As the lights go up, there's not a dry eye in the Olive Branch. Each settler has received a blessing. They walk home in silence. The bright stars shine, each in its own place. And the settlers' hearts are strangely warmed by the thought that in the Mayor's great scheme of things, law and order reign supreme.

HOLY SPIRIT—BUFFALO HUNTER

In Pioneer Theology the Holy Spirit is the Buffalo Hunter. The pioneers call him Wild Red. "Wild," because no one can tell what he'll do next. "Red," because he has red hair.

Wild Red is awesome. He's huge. The strongest guy around. His old buffalo-hide clothes smell like the creature that last wore 'em. Red takes a bath in the creek at least once a month, whether he needs it or not.

There isn't much he can't do. He can hit a spittoon at 20 paces. He can shoot the eye out of the ace of spades. He can break a buffalo without once dusting his pants. Tough? An eight-foot diamond-back once bit Old Red. Nothing could be done to save the snake. It died.

Red ate barbecued rattler that night. Snakes keep their distance now. Yep, the Buffalo Hunter is mighty wild, mighty tough. Tame him? Never!

The Buffalo Hunter's job is to furnish fresh meat for the pioneers each day. Pioneers get mighty hungry. Without Wild Red they'd wither up and blow away like tumbleweeds.

Wild Red has a weird sense of humor. He is always pulling something on somebody. At night, when it's quiet in camp and the pioneers are trying to sleep, Red creeps up and gives someone the hotfoot. There's no rest when he's around.

The settlers live in mortal dread of Red. Wild Red can't resist shaking up the settlers. Sometimes he sneaks up on them. Other times he rides full speed ahead into town on his half-tame buffalo named Pentecost. Red and Pentecost are quite a pair. With Pentecost snortin' and runnin' full blast and Red hollerin' like a madman, who can blame the settlers for being scared?

The Buffalo Hunter's favorite prank is to sneak up on the settlers while they're having an ice cream party. Each Sunday morning, at precisely 11 o'clock, the settlers have an ice cream party on the courthouse lawn. Wild Red ties Pentecost out of sight, then sneaks up behind one of the oak trees. When everyone is real quiet, thinking about that great ice cream party in the sky, Red fires a blast from his big, black buffalo gun. The tremendous explosion shakes the courthouse. The settlers jump out of their skin. Women scream. Dogs bark. The Mayor is roused from his nap.

Chuckling to himself, the Buffalo Hunter then rides through the streets shooting up the town.

One day he almost went too far. He rode old Pentecost right into the Olive Branch. The poor settlers were scared silly. Miss Dove was swinging from a chandelier, screaming for the Sheriff. Poor Norman hid under the bar. While Pentecost was turning over the tables, Wild Red blasted a few milk bottles and rode out, right through the plate glass window. No one rightly knows where the Sheriff was during the commotion, but rumor has it he was hiding under his desk.

At night, Red likes to sit around singing in his deep voice and playing his squeeze box. His song stirs the pioneers.

(Tune: "Onward Christian Soldiers")

Back in Old Jerusalem
Lived a guy named Paul
Hog-tied like a dogie
To the Hebrew law
Then a dream from heaven
Came to set him right
Now he dines with Gentiles
Eatin' pork on Friday night.

(Refrain here)

Down through all the ages
Men have been inspired

By my troubling presence
Burning like a fire
Augustine and Luther
Kierkegaard and Barth
How 'bout John the twenty-third
For giving us new heart!

(Refrain here)

So come on you settlers
Pack up all your gear
Leave your stuffy city
Be a pioneer
Hear the Trail Boss calling
March at his command
New life can be yours if you will
Get up off your can.

Refrain:

I'm the buffalo hunter
Riding through this land
With my big black shotgun
Firmly in my hand.

BISHOP—BANK PRESIDENT

In Settler Theology the bishop is the Bank President. P. Horace Bland, III, chief executive of Settler City National, is easy to spot. He's the only guy in town with a manicure. Also, he drives the only black surrey with a fringe on top. P. Horace dresses like a true easterner. He wears a blue suit and purple vest. His shoes are always shined. He wears a diamond stickpin in the middle—precisely in the middle—of his tie.

Yes, Mr. Bland is impressive. He should be. He represents the great tradition of banking. It is evident to all settlers who diligently read *The Almanac* and listen to the old-timers that from the first settlements there have been bank presidents, tellers, and janitors.

P. Horace is all business. He tolerates no foolishness. His manner is firm, authoritarian. As he says, "Customers respect strength." Holding such a responsible position, the Bank President is always anxious about his image. He cultivates an air of self-confidence. His very presence is reassuring to the settlers. Some go so far as to say he and the Mayor actually look alike.

The Bank President is a busy man. He protects the money, supervises the tellers, presides over the executive board, pacifies customers, and, most importantly, opens new accounts.

P. Horace, working hand in hand with the Sheriff, guards the settlers' treasure. His title is "Defender of the Bank." His job is dangerous. Roaming the territory are notorious outlaws, desperate men who threaten the customers' valuables. The safe has been cracked by such rogues as Black Barth, Two-Gun Tillich, the Niebuhr Boys, and, most dangerous of all, Bullet Man. Once Bullet Man was caught trying to dynamite the upper story of the courthouse. The settlers were about to string him up when his old friend, Herman Neudick, came to the rescue.

No, the Bank President can't be too careful. That's why he has the Sheriff check out strangers.

President Bland supervises the tellers and janitors (deacons). When he hollers, they jump. He believes in being firm with his employees. He tolerates no insubordination. The tellers live on peanuts. But Horace likes it that way. He says, "We know they are working out of dedication, and not for money." Horace watches the tellers like a hawk. Their records are checked daily.

Undas Non Facet

↑
Latin for "Don't make waves"

How much did they take in? Any new customers? Any complaints against them? P. Horace wants his men to look spotless so that the bank can maintain its respectable image.

Bland is president of the bank's executive board. The executive board is made up of a few rich settlers and a few elderly tellers. To qualify for board membership, a customer must be over 60 and have a big account. Tellers must have worked at least 30 years and have unblemished records. Their absolute loyalty to the bank must be beyond doubt. The executive board is the policy-making body. And it does make policy! It makes whatever policy P. Horace tells it to make.

The Bank President's specialty is public relations. He knows the family history of each big depositor. Even in his sleep he can name their grandchildren.

He keeps a secret file on his tellers. Troublemakers must be dismissed quickly and quietly. Bland tries to get on the ground floor of any new real estate deals in town. He has a nose for gold like an old prospector.

The crowning joy of Bland's day is opening new accounts. He insists on doing it personally. Opening new accounts is called "the laying on of hands."

Bland puts on quite a show, but he's a tenderfoot inside. A dude like Bland wouldn't last two days on the trail. He acts tough within the safe confines of the bank walls, but when it comes to trailblazing, he's a greenhorn.

President Bland is usually reserved, but at precisely 2 p.m., when the bank closes, he pulls down the shade and leads his employees in song. His whiskey tenor voice soars high and free as he drowns out the others with his favorite song:

(Tune: "Bringing in the Sheaves")

Bringing in the greenbacks
Raising lots of money
New vaults we'll be needing
Tellers don't ya' see?
Business we're a'drumming
Customers are coming
Makes ya' feel like humming
Bringing in the sheaves.

(Refrain)

Sharpen up the book work
Keep our records spotless
Settler City National
Must like clockwork run
We will try all measures
To get on our ledgers
Lots of tithing pledgers
Bringing in the sheaves.

(Refrain)

When ol' Gabriel blows that
Bugle for the Mayor

When we hear his blessing
"Bankers you've done well"
Angels will be winging
Golden bells a'ringing
Then you'll hear us singing
Bringing in the sheaves.

(Refrain)

Refrain:

Bringing in the sheaves
Bringing in the sheaves
Customers we're thanking
Bringing in the sheaves

Bringing in the sheaves
Bringing in the sheaves
O the joy of banking
Bringing in the sheaves

While each denominational town has a bank president, in some towns the presidents are not called bishops. But just as there is a visible and an invisible church, so also there are visible and invisible bishops.

BISHOP—DISHWASHER

In Pioneer Theology the bishop is the Dishwasher. He is the servant of the Cook, who, in turn, is the servant of the pioneers.

The wagon train has always needed Dishwashers. Dishwashing goes way back to the days when "Rock" was around. Old Peter Rock was quite a guy. Rumor is that he was the first Dishwasher appointed by Josh himself.

The Dishwasher's name is Willard Dingman. Will is a big man, over six feet. Though he doesn't like to brag, he's the strongest pioneer in camp. He's also the most patient. Will has keen eyes and ears. He can smell trouble brewing before anyone else can. He's the first to help when the wagons get stuck, or the Cook needs a hand, or when ruffled feelings need soothing. Will works hard. He doesn't want anything to slow the pioneer's progress.

Will has the most humble job on the wagon train. He does the dirty work so that the Cook can keep his mind on the cooking. The Dishwasher gathers wood, makes the fire, helps the Cook prepare the meal, and scrubs the pots and pans. The Cook, of course, gets most of the credit for good meals. But the Dishwasher doesn't mind. He says, "Just so the pioneers have good grub and strength for the trail." But the Cook knows Old Will is the key to good eatin'.

Even though Will has a humble job, he doesn't gripe. Pioneers are funny like that. No one cares who gets the glory as long as the job gets done. And the pioneers have a strange way of showing honor. On the wagon train, he is greatest who serves most.

Will's dishpan hands are his mark of status. Not everyone makes it "up" the ladder to this greater servant role.

The Cook and Dishwasher are equal partners in pioneering. Together they plan the menu, cook, serve meals, clean up. While riding on the chuck wagon, they relish talking about past adventures and they plan for the days ahead.

Usually the Cook and Dishwasher are peace-loving men, but when their fellow pioneers are attacked, they fight like a papa grizzly. Let some bushwhacker try to stop the wagon train and *pow!*

When lead starts flying, the Cook and Dishwasher look out for each other. Occasionally Billy James and some of his settler vigilantes hanker to have some fun at the Cook's expense, or Dr. Billy rides in and tries to sell his Cure-All Tonic as a substitute for the thrill of pioneering.

When that happens, the intruders spend the next three days picking buckshot out of their bottoms. Will doesn't miss with his double-barreled 12-gauge.

But usually Will is a good-natured cuss. The pioneers like him and the Cook couldn't do without him. He whistles while he butchers the meat Wild Red has brought in. He keeps the coffee pot going day and night.

Will is a wise old pot-wrangler, and he shares his wisdom with those who are smart enough to listen.

CLERGYMAN—TELLER

In Settler Theology the clergyman is the Teller, Mr. Melvin O. Patsy. Melvin is nice. He wears a blue suit and maroon tie. He has a handkerchief tucked neatly in his coat pocket.

Melvin is pale. Tellers don't get much sunshine. And, of course, he is clean-shaven. P. Horace knows how settlers feel about beards. (Only saddle tramps and outlaws wear beards.) Mr. Patsy is a soft-spoken man, as are all Tellers. They speak in a "bank tone."

Not every settler has what it takes to be a Teller. A Teller must be a settler's settler. He is custodian of all the valuables of Settler City. Think of the responsibility! The settlers must be darn sure that *their* Teller, even if he should get the pioneer itch, won't budge.

So Melvin was thrilled when he got the Mayor's call. The Mayor himself, working through his close friend, the Bank President, appoints all Tellers. You don't just *decide* to become a Teller, you must be *called!*

Melvin O. Patsy stays busy. His main job is receiving deposits. He also keeps detailed records. At least 75% of a Teller's job is bookkeeping. He has to keep up with new customers, deposits, withdrawals, loans, mortgages, safety deposit boxes—you name it. When P. Horace comes around, the books must balance—or else!

Public relations is another important part of Melvin's job. P. Horace is always quoting his favorite limerick to the Tellers:

> *There was a young Teller named Pete*
> *Whose conduct was less than discreet.*

So P. Horace Bland
Got rid of this man.
He's now selling brooms on the street.

Bland's limerick is a stern reminder to the Tellers. They dare not forget banking's No. 1 rule—"DON'T OFFEND THE CUS- TOMERS." Not once in 20 years has Melvin forgotten to gargle before coming to work.

Though being a Teller is a high calling, Melvin's life is not easy. He has no say in how the bank is run. The President calls the shots. A "Teller's cage" is not called that for nothing.

Another problem is money. Tellers are poor, but they never grumble. They look at it this way: Since they are helping pro- tect the settlers' valuables, they are really working for the Mayor himself and not just for their boss, the Bank President. If such a noble calling doesn't pay well, why complain?

Besides, Tellers get by; their wives can always take in washing.

Most Tellers are married. The Bank President doesn't like single Tellers. Bachelor Tellers often get into, shall we say, "unteller-like" situations.

Besides, if the customers like them, the Tellers are given turnip greens and other nice things. They get discounts in some stores. Melvin has to live in a bank-owned house, but he doesn't mind. Like he says, "It's all for the Mayor."

The toughest part of the Teller's job is pleasing two bosses at the same time. Melvin must please both the Bank President and the customers.

To displease one is usually to encounter the wrath of the other. For some strange reason, the President is closer to the customers than to the Tellers, even though they are his employees. Maybe the President understands that it's the customers' money that keeps the bank in business.

Once upon a time a Teller got a fancy notion about improving working conditions. The young whippersnapper organized a Teller's association. Well, sir, Old P. Horace got wind of it. The radical young Teller got sent to a ghost town, a place called Cactus Station.

No one in Settler City has heard from the young feller since. Some say the Courthouse Committee on Un-settler Activities did him in.

No, Melvin's life is not easy, but he doesn't mind. He knows that a pot of gold ultimately awaits Tellers who persevere.

CLERGYMAN—COOK

In Pioneer Theology the clergyman is the Cook. His job is to dish up the meat provided by the Buffalo Hunter.

"Hot Sauce" Smith is as strong as a mule—he has to be if he's to feed famished pioneers three times a day.

Hot Sauce, as the nickname suggests, is not famous for bland cooking. He puts zest into life. Hot Sauce loves the trail. Cooks are that way. Like all pioneers, they sometimes get weary and discouraged, but once cooking gets in their blood, they're hooked.

Hot Sauce, like his friend Wild Red, is always up to mischief. He delights in keeping the pioneers on their toes. He isn't above sneaking up on a sleeping pioneer and clanging a couple of pie tins. But Hot Sauce isn't mean. He takes good care of his fellow pioneers. There's no gravel in *his* beans.

Hot Sauce is an artist with garlic and red pepper. He takes the buffalo meat Wild Red brings him, adds his own spices, and rings the bell. When the pioneers taste his grub, they know they've had something!

Many of the recipes Hot Sauce uses have been handed down from one generation of Cooks to another. But Hot Sauce often surprises the pioneers with a new dish. "Can't let their taste buds retire," he thinks. "Makes 'em think about what they're eating." New recipes bring out the settler in some pioneers. They say, "This ain't no good 'cause I never tasted it before." But Hot Sauce just smiles and goes on with his cooking.

He takes pride in seeing that the pioneers are well fed and makes sure that they eat their share of mustard greens, even though they grumble. Hot Sauce knows it's his job to keep the pioneers healthy. If they grumble—they grumble.

Once a week the pioneers feast. It's the high point of a hard week on the trail. At the feast the pioneers gather like a family united by a purpose. They talk about the meaning of life on the trail, share their secret fears, confess that they often act like a bunch of settlers.

They listen again to the Scout's stories. They learn that they, too, can move out, fear or no fear. As the pioneers share the bread and wine of the feast, the Cook reminds them that though the trail has been rough, tomorrow is a new and promising day. A new day to blaze trails, to heed the demands of the Trail Boss, to follow Josh over mountains and through valleys, to trust that they will be fed by Wild Red himself. After the feast the pioneers have their dance, a real wing-ding!

The pioneers couldn't make it without the big feast. The mountains, the burning sand, the storms make the pioneers long for the comforts back East. The feast renews their strength and vision. That is why Hot Sauce takes such pride in preparing a good feast.

Food for the pioneers! That's what it's all about for Hot Sauce, the Cook, and Will, the Dishwasher. The chuck wagon brings up the rear of the wagon train, but the Cook and Dishwasher don't mind working behind the scenes.

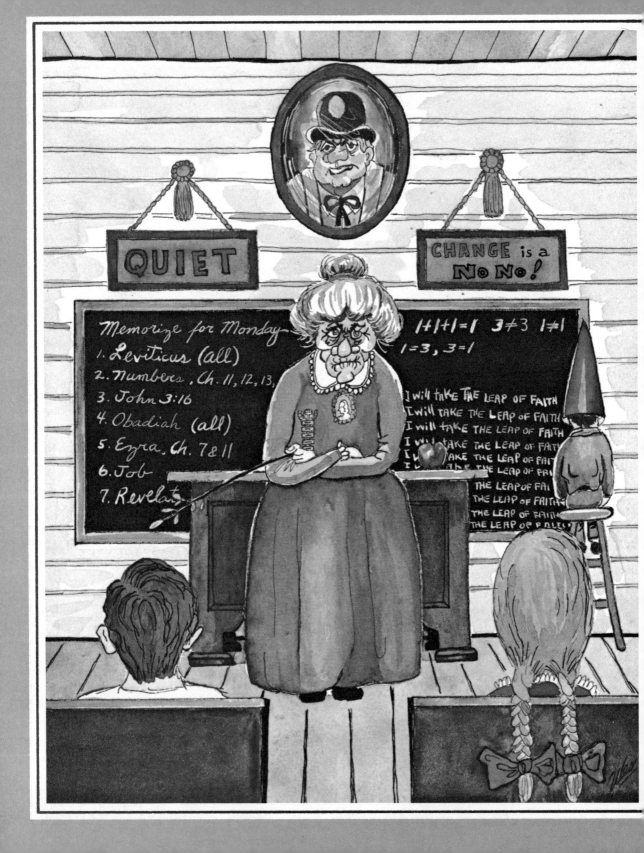

COURTHOUSE DOGMATICS

Courthouse Dogmatics is an outline of the eternal verities of Settler
City. Settler City youngsters must memorize it before
being brought to the Bank President to open an account.
Here are some of the main items.

Anti-Christ. Anyone wishing to impeach the Sheriff.

Ascension. The time the Sheriff went upstairs to the Mayor's office
to get his badge.

Atonement. The Sheriff taking the rap so the Mayor won't string up
all the naughty settlers.

Beatific vision. The Honorable Alpha O. Mega, standing in the
window of his second-story office, eating ice cream.

Churchmanship. Hanging around the courthouse. Making all the
ice cream parties. Taking a turn cranking the freezer.

Eternal life. Escape from Boot Hill. (Synonyms: Golden Ranch in
the Sky, Sweet By-and-By, the Hereafter, Happy Hunting
Ground.)

Eternity. What starts after you die.

Ethics. The rules on file in the Mayor's office. (Copies are posted on
the bulletin board in the Sheriff's office and on the door
of the Olive Branch.)

Faith. Believing that the Mayor (who never shows his face) is in the
courthouse. Counting on the Sheriff to protect you.

Freedom. The choice between keeping your nose clean or getting thrown in the hoosegow. (This word is basically a Pioneer concept. Settlers rarely use it.)

Gospel. Alpha O. Mega so loved Settler City that he sent his only Sheriff to secure the town. Those who believe this will some day wind up on that Great Golden Ranch in the Sky.

Grace. Getting off the hook. The Sheriff softening up the Mayor.

Heaven. Security.

Hell. Life outside the ease, comfort, and protection of Settler City.

Heresy. Making waves. Saying the Mayor's rules are wrong. Doubting Settler sayings.

Holy. The opposite of naughty.

Image of God. The "safety first" spirit.

Incarnation. Believing Miss Dove is one of the Sheriff's parents.

Kingdom of God. Settler City.

Laity. Settlers. Bank customers. Those Settlers with less status than the boys in the bank.

Prayer. Settlers telling the Mayor what they want done.

Religion. Manipulation. Like a rooster who believes his crowing brings the sun up, the Settlers believe their rituals "make it happen."

Resurrection. The Sheriff walking out of Boot Hill. Alpha O. Mega's final triumph over outside agitators.

Revelation. The notices on the Sheriff's bulletin board. Information whispered in your ear by Miss Dove. The exact words of *The Almanac.*

Salvation. Living in the restful shade of the courthouse lawn.

Sin. Committing a Settler City no-no. Being naughty.

Theology. The Settler City Organization Chart, engraved in gold and kept in the bank vault.

The Trinity. The Mayor makes the rules; the Sheriff enforces them; the Saloon Girl helps Settlers forget their troubles. Three peas in a pod.

Unforgivable sin. Wishing the Olive Branch would close and Miss Dove would be run out of town. (Don't worry, any Settler would melt in his boots at the thought of losing Miss Dove.)

TALES OF THE TRAIL

This is the Buffalo Hunter's diary. It is a collection of Pioneer insights. Being a diary it is open-ended. Wild Red reads the TALES OF THE TRAIL around the evening campfire.

Anti-Christ. Anyone who tries to turn the Pioneers around by saying east is west and west is east. One who thinks the sun sets in the east.

Ascension. The time J. Hova called Josh up the mountain to see the whole frontier. From that point on, the Pioneers have known that J. Hova and Josh share the same vision and ride together.

Atonement. Josh whipping all the powers of Settler City and blazing the Pioneer trail himself. Opening the trail to all men.

Beatific vision. J. Hova looking west.

Churchmanship. Doing the chores necessary to keep the wagons rolling. Everything from greasing axles to settling feuds between pioneers.

Eternal life. Knowing J. Hova as Trail Boss. Following Josh. The realization that the depth and meaning of life IS pioneering. (Not to be confused with the Sweet By-and-By and other Settler City Funeral Parlor talk.)

Eternity. What J. Hova is. The depth and meaning of time.

Ethics. Figuring out and doing what pioneering demands.

Faith. The spirit of adventure. The decision, in response to J. Hova's call, to risk your life on the trail.

Freedom. What it's all about. Being yourself and giving yourself to J. Hova's great pioneering adventure and its demands.

Gospel. J. Hova's complete acceptance of all men, Pioneers and Settlers alike. The existence of the wagon train is, in itself, good news. The news that reality is "pioneer-like."

Grace. The power that frees men to be Pioneers. Both the voice and fist of J. Hova.

Heaven. Riding close to J. Hova.

Hell. The mule-headed decision to be a Settler come hell or high water.

Heresy. (This is almost always a Settler word.)

Holy. Western! Great! Wow!

Image of God. The Pioneer itch.

Incarnation. J. Hova's words "Move out!" embodied in Josh. Knowing Josh is a chip off the old block.

Kingdom of God. The invisible bond uniting all Pioneers. The frontier character of the whole universe. J. Hova, through Josh, dealing the cards.

Laity. Those, other than Cooks and Dishwashers, who are obedient to the voice of the Trail Boss. The first wave of civilization.

Prayer. Being open to the glory and demands of pioneering. Listening to the voice of the Trail Boss within the everyday demands of the wagon train.

Religion. Celebration. The dance of life. The Pioneer's dramatic response to J. Hova, Josh, and Wild Red.

Resurrection. J. Hova's decisive victory over settlerdom. The Scout leading those who die to Settler life into the thrill of Pioneer life. Knowing Pioneer life is the final meaning of life.

Revelation. J. Hova's commands. Knowing J. Hova is the Trail Boss. Everything that happens on the trail.

Salvation. Trusting J. Hova and following Josh while living on meat provided by Wild Red.

Sin. Deciding to turn back.

Theology. The daily log of the wagon train.

Trinity. J. Hova made and maintains the wagons; Josh leads the way; Wild Red sustains the Pioneers. But the three are one in purpose and spirit.

Unforgivable sin. Saying Wild Red is a Settler in disguise. (But don't worry; anyone who has ever rubbed noses with Wild Red wouldn't dream of saying something so stupid.)

CHRISTIAN

CHRISTIAN—SETTLERS

In Settler Theology the Christian is the Settler (naturally). The Settler fears the open, unknown frontier. He lives for the Last Roundup when he can join the Settlers Triumphant* at that Great Golden Ranch in the sky.

The Settler's goal is to keep in good with the Mayor and stay out of the Sheriff's way. He keeps his money in the bank because he doesn't want to offend the Banker. "Better safe than sorry," he says.

*Settlers Triumphant are dead Settlers. Settlers Militant are breathing Settlers. (Dead Settlers are referred to as Settlers Triumphant because death is the ultimate in "Settlerhood." As Whittlin' Willie, the town philosopher, says, "You don't have to change none when you're dead.")

The Settler is awed by the courthouse, which symbolizes security, order, stability, safety. Indeed, the whitewashed courthouse is a symbol of Settler City.

Settlers are not all alike, though they do have one thing in common—they ain't goin' no place. Different Settlers love Settler City for different reasons. Percy Sims, who runs the general store, likes Settler City because he always knows where he stands. He makes his profit and loss statement each day, takes his money to the bank, and hits the sack by 8:30 p.m. There's no guesswork to life in Settler City.

Big George, the blacksmith, likes the Sheriff's way of doing things. He loves laws. "Laws are like anvils," he says. "They don't break and they don't change. Give me the anvil life."

Then there's poor harmless Uncle Eddie. What would he do without the protection of Settler City? Uncle Eddie stays high on Dr. Billy's tonic; he's been on it for as long as anybody can remember. Without the security of Settler City and the comfort of Dr. Billy's tonic, Old Eddie simply wouldn't make it.

And how about Miss Henrietta Clementine Jones? After 47 years in the Settler City library, Miss Jones would be lost on the trail. What would she do without her books—and her daydreams?

Yes, Settler City is "home" for many persons and for different reasons.

But in spite of their differences, settlers rarely fuss—at least, they don't feud in the open. Settlers, no matter how they feel, must be polite at all times. They learn to be nice while they're no higher than daddy's boots.

Still, in Settler City it's every man for himself. Settlers try to outshine each other, though on the surface it's all sweetness and light. Generally, settlers don't even know each other. They're scared to reveal themselves.

Life in Settler City is boring. Bored people gossip. If a Settler wants to protect his position in the community, he has to watch what he says. The NO EXPLORATION rule isn't aimed solely at keeping Settlers off the frontier; it's meant to keep Settlers from becoming too chummy with each other, too.

How does the town hang together, then? Simple. With three golden cords: fear of the frontier, obedience to the Mayor, and, strongest of all, inertia.

The Settlers' relationship with the pioneers and other riffraff can be summed up in one word—NONE. Settlers have nothing to do with pioneers if they can help it. You can't blame them. Pioneers are always telling the Settlers about the thrill of pioneer life and asking them to join the train. This is upsetting.

Settlers believe in organization. The organization chart in the Mayor's office is a sight to behold. Everyone is on it. The chart looks like a pyramid. On top is, guess who? The Honorable Alpha O. Mega and his sidekicks, the Sheriff and Miss Dove. They are like three peas in a pod. They have absolute control. Next comes the Bank President, then the Tellers and Janitors, and finally, the run-of-the-mill Settlers. The Mayor and Bank President say, "Our job is a 'tellin'; their job is a 'listenin'."

Life in Settler City isn't *all* dull. Each Sunday morning, there's that ice cream party on the courthouse lawn. The rule against walking on the lawn is suspended. The party is quite pleasant if Wild Red and Pentecost don't show up. The Settlers eat fried chicken, sing folk songs, read from *The Almanac,* and talk about the good old days. Good Settlers never miss an ice cream party; they feel they owe it to the Mayor to be there.

The high point of the party is when the Settlers stand, like a herd of sheep, and proudly say in unison the Settler's Creed:

SETTLER'S CREED

The Mayor's in the courthouse
Of this I'm quite convinced
'Cause if he ain't a' running things
Then life don't make no sense.

The Sheriff's keepin' order
In this our Settler town
He helps old ladies cross the street
And puts the bad guys down.

The Olive Branch is comfort
To those in need of love
Alleluia praise the Sheriff
For sending us Miss Dove.

O how we stick together
It's OK if we fall
When we get out of old Boot Hill
O, won't we have a ball.

Then the Settlers sing their closing hymn:

BLESSED INSURANCE

(Tune: "Blessed Assurance")
Blessed insurance I've got it made
The Sheriff has my policy paid
Isn't it nice to just sit around
Under the shade trees in Settler Town.

(Refrain)

Listening to the coos of Miss Dove
Waiting to go to that land up above
Keeping my nose clean being so pure
When you're a good guy life is secure.

(Refrain)

Refrain:
This is my story, this is my dream
To be a'resting eating ice cream
This is my story, this is my dream
To be a'resting eating ice cream.

There are a number of worthy organizations found in Settler City.

For men there's the W.A.S.P. Lodge, which is always sponsoring interesting diversions like a midnight ride or the Miss Settler City Contest.

Pioneers Anonymous try to keep from succumbing to the pioneer itch. Some are former pioneers who kicked the habit but are tempted to take it up again; others are malcontents who occasionally want to run away from it all. Together, they drink coffee and talk about the advantages of the comfortable life. Soon they're okay again.

The Courthouse Guild is made up of ladies who do helpful things like setting up the picnic tables at the ice cream party, washing the table cloths, and polishing the silverware. The Sisters of the Sheriff tend the flowers in the Sheriff's window box. (The women of Settler City stay in the background; it isn't ladylike to nose around in the menfolks' business.)

The Young Settlers League trains the youth. The members study *The Almanac* and witness how they've surrendered to the Sheriff. They are allowed to go to the Olive Branch on Wednesday nights to hear Miss Dove's sweet song, which always brings tears. The high point of the year is the Annual Y.S.L. Essay Contest. Hubert Heartmoore won this year's contest with his essay, "Why I Am Proud To Be A Settler." It was published on the front page of the town's newspaper, the Silent Settler. The young people are kept busy, but their advice is never sought. In Settler City folks believe children should be seen but not heard.

Yes, Settler City has something for everybody. The town may be dull, but it's not dangerous. Unless the Mayor calls him prematurely, a Settler is pretty likely to live his three score and ten and die in bed an undisturbed man.

CHRISTIAN—PIONEER

In Pioneer Theology the Christian is the Pioneer. A man of risk and daring, boundless curiosity, and wild imagination.

The Pioneer is tougher than a longhorn steak. He has to be. The trail is hot and dusty. Hours are long, saddles hard. Working with range critters ain't easy.

The Pioneer has no romantic dude notions about life on the trail. Each day's travel takes him farther into the unknown. Wagons get stuck. Pioneers squabble. No, Pioneer life is not for the guy who wants cheap thrills.

Pioneering is for keeps. It demands everything. It promises only LIFE. Not pleasure. Not success. Lots of townfolk daydream about becoming Pioneers, but most of them never get past Miss Dove's Olive Branch. If you want to be a Pioneer, you've got to buckle on your spurs and six-shooter and GO.

The Pioneer life is aimed, like a rifle, at the future. Although the Pioneer respects the past, he moves toward tomorrow. He wants to be where the action is. He uses lessons of the past to create a better future.

The Pioneer doesn't wander around like a lost calf. Where the Trail Boss points, he goes—in a straight line (until the Trail Boss sights a new direction). The Pioneer doesn't mess around, but he considers no trails off-limits. You might say a Pioneer is willing to go anywhere, but his footprints run straight.

Everyone is welcome on the wagon train. The Pioneer isn't a snooty critter. If you're going west, you're welcome. Cattlemen and sheepmen ride together behind the Trail Boss.

The Pioneer's life is hard, but he enjoys himself. On the wild and woolly frontier, there's a new adventure at every turn. There's always something to share, if it's only to work together fixing a wagon wheel. There's the coffee pot on the open fire. Pioneers really live it up! Just try to find a Pioneer who would give up the trail. You might as well look for a pink armadillo with purple spots.

Where does a guy get the Pioneer itch? What happens that frees a man so that he can turn his back on the normal, guaranteed—and boring—life? It's hard to say. It's a little different for each man.

Some are repelled by the dullness of Settler City. Knowing everything before it happens. Always stuffing yourself into the sausage grinder of niceness. Being what somebody else wants you to be. Living and dying without screaming a little. It's the Mayor and his system, the Sheriff and his laws, Miss Dove and her calf eyes and cane-syrup voice.

Others are drawn by the wide open spaces. Places where no one has been before. The unknown. A new land that will be changed in part as a man himself is changed. Clean air, room to stretch. A land where there is challenge—even danger. The kind that thrills the soul.

And always there is the voice of the Trail Boss. The voice that makes no sound. The voice that is loudest in the still of night. The voice that says "life" where only death can be seen. The voice that says "hope" where there is no hope. The voice that says "courage" when fear chills to the bone.

Then there's the Scout. The one who has been there. Who rides ahead. Who blazes the trail. Ol' Josh—a life without fences. What a guy! You say it can't be done? Hell, man, Josh did it!

And just when you know you can't take one more step, not one, blam! Wild Red (with the aid of his six-shooter) makes you dance. Wild Red laughs while his gun blazes. The body can dance when its owner thought it couldn't even move!

Trade all that for the nice, sure, safe, secure boredom of Settler City? Not a chance. Not for a Pioneer.

There are no Lone Rangers on the trail. Pioneering is too tough for that. Moving a wagon train isn't easy, so the Pioneers count on each other. Each man has to make the lonely decision of whether or not to leave Settler City, but once on the trail, each person is equally important. That's why the heroes (if there are any) are the ones who serve most.

Settler women are hothouse plants. They are confined to pedestals behind the scenes. Not Pioneer women! Pioneering is too demanding to fool around with Settler notions about "a woman's place." Pioneer women are in on every aspect of the westward journey. A pioneer woman must be able to handle a team of mules as well as a man, and shoot as straight as a man. Some of the pioneer cooks are women.

Pioneer men and women share, plan, and work together

as a team. The pioneer women have no special women's organizations. No need for them. Pioneer men and women have a common vision and a common task—moving west.

Young people aren't second-class citizens either. They learn the ways of the West and do their share in keeping the wagons moving.

No, the Pioneer isn't a lone coyote. Pioneers aren't all alike, nor do they all like each other. But they are held together by a common vision, a common task, and, when necessary, a little buckshot from the Buffalo Hunter's sawed-off shotgun. Conformity, no! Unity of purpose, yes!

The Pioneer spirit is a driving force on the wagon train. It's hard to describe, but Pioneer spirit is a mixture of humility, gratitude, compassion, freedom, and, most important, joy.

The Pioneer is humble. Not in the weak, "excuse me for livin'" sense. He is humble because he shapes his life in response to the call of the Trail Boss, the demands of the trail, and the daily needs of the wagon train.

The Pioneer is grateful. Thankful for life itself. Thankful for the chance to move into the unknown. Thankful for daily strength, and yes, even for his weaknesses. (That always throws Settlers.) The Pioneer expresses his gratitude by opening himself to the needs of those around him.

The Pioneer is a man of compassion. Compassion is strong, not weak. It's not like Miss Dove's song. Compassion is like a blacksmith's hammer on white-hot metal. Compassion is the power that sets men free. Compassion is the power of one life making another life strong. Compassion is the Pioneer's challenge to the Settler: "MOVE OUT!" It is also tender care for those who are weak. Compassion is blazing trails for others to follow, even being faithful to those yet unborn.

The Pioneer is free. Not like a hermit, but rather free to be and do with others without becoming just another member of the herd.

Pioneer freedom is the ability to cross high mountains and wide rivers, to look as far as the eye can see and know that the space out there is all for you. And to know that the space within your soul is still greater than all you've seen.

Pioneer freedom is freedom to face the Settler within each of us.

The Pioneer is a man of joy. Not settler-type happiness, which is merely the absence of pain. But deep joy. The joy that comes through a lifetime of living exposed to the raw elements. A life with nothing fenced out. The joy of knowing you've lived without holding back. The joy that comes when you can be afraid without being afraid of your fears. The joy of living beyond the confines of winning and losing, success and failure. Of knowing that "yes" means yes and "no" means no, but both mean LIFE. The thrill of the trail is following a Trail Boss who himself is all the possible frontiers and who, within himself, moves beyond each horizon.

The pioneer sounds like a great guy, doesn't he? Well, he is but one must not forget the dangers of pioneering—inner dangers.

One of these is "Echo Canyon." At one time or another every pioneer goes through the dangerous, narrow pass. In Echo Canyon one's own voice is magnified and returns as an echo. Many a pioneer has listened to his own booming voice as it bounces off the canyon wall and returns to him.

"Ah," he thinks to himself, "the Trail Boss is talking to me." When a pioneer mistakes his own voice for the voice of the Trail Boss, his hat suddenly seems to start shrinking. His brain seems to be getting larger.

"Who needs the Trail Boss?" he says. "Since the Trail Boss is talking directly to me, I can lead the wagons."

"Follow me," he shouts. "I know the way." Many a proud pioneer has led many a foolish pioneer on a wild armadillo chase.

Another inner danger is the "Westerner Than Thou" attitude. Preoccupied with his own journey, the arrogant pioneer looks down on his fellow pioneers. He forgets the Scout is the chief pioneer and all other pioneers are brothers. He tries to pass other wagons so his will be the farthest west at all times. He resents being behind another wagon.

A third peril is hankering to ride one of the wild mustangs called High Horses. The pioneer who starts riding a High Horse glories more in *being* a pioneer than in *moving* into the unknown future. This poor fellow forgets that the thrill of discovery and adventure is its own reward. Instead, he boasts to himself and others about the superiority of the pioneer life, and has contempt rather than compassion for settlers.

No pioneer can afford to forget that the pioneer spirit is a gift and not a possession. And he dare not assume that the settler is completely dead in him. It is by the call of the Trail Boss, the leading of the Scout, and the daily sustenance of the Buffalo Hunter that a pioneer is what he is.

But these inner dangers shouldn't discourage anyone from hitting the trail. Because pioneers who get lost in Echo Canyon or one of the other pitfalls along the trail will soon be brought back to their senses by good ol' Wild Red and his shotgun. Besides, the trail is worth all the trials, inner or outer.

As the Pioneer's Creed says:

The Trail Boss is a'ridin' hard
He's strong and wild and tough
He calls to us to move out too
Although the trail is rough.

Josh is up front leading us
Far out beyond the line
Where chicken hearts turn back in fear
Security to find.

Wild Red screams his rebel yell
The settlers think he's nuts
But in his strange delightful way
He gives the Pioneers guts.

Come all Pioneers ride out now
New deserts we must cross
Put all your trust in life or death
In our glorious Trail Boss.

Well, pardner, there it is.
Make up your mind,
put it on the line.
The wagon is moving out.

WESTERN THEOLOGY

Written and illustrated by Wes Seeliger

Foreword by Keith Miller

There are two views of life and two kinds of people. Some see life as a possession to be carefully guarded. They are SETTLERS. Others see life as a fantastic, wild, explosive gift. They are PIONEERS.

Their theology is as different as their lifestyles. SETTLER THEOLOGY plays it safe. It discourages the asking of questions, worships the status quo, and pays homage to a church that is safe, sane, and self-satisfied.

PIONEER THEOLOGY talks about life and what it means to truly *live*—wildly, dangerously, joyfully! Life on the trail is never dull, and the pioneer knows that being on the "Renewal Or Bust" wagon train led by the Trail Boss (God) is the ultimate adventure.

Seeliger says that "a settler community in a changing world has no future, and that is as it should be. But God will have his pioneer community. The question for us is—will the institutional church be that community of risk and daring? The pioneer spirit *is* alive in the church, and *Western Theology* was written to fan that spark of life, and to call the settler church to move out joyfully into the unknowable future."

Oh, one more thing. *Western Theology* is a satire which may be brilliant for some and "a horrible sacrilege" (as Keith Miller warns in his foreword) for others. Whether you're put off or entranced by the humor, look deeper for the real questions of faith that Seeliger is asking. And then look deeply into yourself and see if there beats the heart of a contented, purring settler or a raring-to-go pioneer.

Wes Seeliger is a tall Texan. With his boots on he can look down on Matt Dillon. His sense of humor is as large as his home state. Wes' specialty is theology people can understand; only the weariest of settlers can sleep through his sermons.

The trail for Wes began in 1938 in Lockhart, Texas. He acquired a B.A. degree from The University of Texas (in the process becoming a rabid Longhorn fan) and received his theological education at Southern Methodist University and The Episcopal Theological Seminary of the Southwest.

Wes began his formal ministry at Texas A&M University. Ordained to the priesthood in 1966, he is now rector of The Episcopal Church of The Advent in Houston, Texas.

The book that Keith Miller calls "vivid, stimulating, thought-provoking"

Now for the first time, you can order up extra copies for groups at huge savings.

Great! for seminars
retreats
seminary study
discussion groups
vacation Bible classes
Sunday school programs
for adults and youngsters alike

They make marvelous gifts, too, for the Holidays, birthdays, confirmations, and those other special occasions.

Used and proved valuable . . .

from Southern Baptists . . . to Lutherans . . . to Roman Catholics . . . to the United States Navy's Chaplain Corps.

The whole family, young and old, will enjoy its colorful illustrations and stimulating (if not orthodox) ideas and concepts. WESTERN THEOLOGY will rekindle that delight of faith and ultimately strengthen religious belief by showing Christianity from a new perspective.

Quantity Discount Prices

1 copy	$ 6.95	10 copies	$ 57.50	50 copies	$ 225.00
3 copies	$19.00	20 copies	$110.00	100 copies	$ 425.00
5 copies	$30.00	30 copies	$157.50	500 copies	$1950.00

No Charge for Shipping and Handling!